Frances Lincoln Limited
74–77 White Lion Street
London N1 9PF
www.franceslincoln.com

The Royal Horticultural Society
Wild in the Garden Diary 2015
Copyright © Frances Lincoln Limited 2014
Photographs copyright © individual photographers
as listed in Picture Credits
Text copyright © the Royal Horticultural Society 2014
and printed under licence granted by the Royal Horticultural
Society, Registered Charity number 222879/SC038262.
For more information visit our website or call 0845 130 4646.
An interest in gardening is all you need to enjoy being a
member of the RHS.
Website: www.rhs.org.uk

First Frances Lincoln edition 2014

Astronomical information © Crown Copyright. Reproduced by
permission of the Controller of Her Majesty's Stationery Office
and the UK Hydrographic Office (www.ukho.gov.uk)

A catalogue record for this book is available
from the British Library

ISBN: 978-0-7112-3513-7

Printed in China

1 2 3 4 5 6 7 8 9

Front cover European Rabbit (*Oryctolagus cuniculus*)
Back cover Harvest Mouse (*Micromys minutus*) immature,
on Lords and Ladies (*Arum maculatum*) fruit.
Introduction Green Lacewing (*Chrysoperla carnea*)
on a corncockle flower.

RHS FLOWER SHOWS 2015

Regrettably Flower Show dates are no longer included in this
diary. Show date changes after publication caused confusion.
The following dates were correct at the time of going to press
but, due to circumstances beyond our control, show dates
often change in the interim period so please confirm before
travelling. Neither the RHS nor the publisher can accept liability
for any errors.

CHELSEA FLOWER SHOW (19–23 May 2015), **HAMPTON
COURT PALACE FLOWER SHOW** (30 June–5 July 2015),
TATTON PARK FLOWER SHOW (22–26 July 2015),
CARDIFF FLOWER SHOW (1–3 May 2015), **MALVERN
SPRING FESTIVAL** (7–10 May 2015), **LONDON SHOWS**
throughout the year.

RHS Flower Show Information can be found by visiting
www.rhs.org.uk

PICTURE CREDITS

All photographs are from The Garden Collection
(www.garden-collection.com)
Kim Taylor Introduction, Week 5, Week 24; **Roger Tidman/
FLPA** Back cover; **Andrew Parkinson/FLPA** Front cover;
Gianpiero Ferrari/FLPA Week 2, Week 13, Week 48; **Mike
Lane/FLPA** Week 3; **David T. Grewcock/FLPA** Week 4; **Erica
Olsen/FLPA** Week 7; **Paul Miguel/FLPA** Week 8; **Des Ong/
FLPA** Week 9, Week 25, Week 34; **Roger Wilmshurst/FLPA**
Week 11; **Martin Hughes-Jones** Week 12; **Phil McLean/FLPA**
Week 14; **Chris Mattison/FLPA** Week 16; **Gary K Smith/
FLPA** Week 17; **Derek Middleton/FLPA** Week 19, Week 39;
Flora Press Week 20, Week 21, Week 38; **Paul Hobson/FLPA**
Week 22, Week 42; **Liz Eddison** Week 26; **Martin B Withers/
FLPA** Week 28; **Malcolm Schuyl/FLPA** Week 29; **Derek
Harris** Week 30, Week 41; **Matt Cole/FLPA** Week 31; **Mike
Powles/FLPA** Week 33; **Paul Sawer/FLPA** Week 35; **Matt
Cole/FLPA** Week 37; **Richard Becker/FLPA** Week 43; **Neil
Sutherland** Week 44; **Jules Cox/FLPA** Week 46, Week 50;
Nicola Stocken Tomkins Week 47; **Mike Lane/FLPA** Week 51,
Week 53; **Modeste Herwig** Week 52

CALENDAR 2015

JANUARY
M	T	W	T	F	S	S
			1	2	3	4
5	6	7	8	9	10	11
12	13	14	15	16	17	18
19	20	21	22	23	24	25
26	27	28	29	30	31	

FEBRUARY
M	T	W	T	F	S	S
						1
2	3	4	5	6	7	8
9	10	11	12	13	14	15
16	17	18	19	20	21	22
23	24	25	26	27	28	

MARCH
M	T	W	T	F	S	S
						1
2	3	4	5	6	7	8
9	10	11	12	13	14	15
16	17	18	19	20	21	22
23	24	25	26	27	28	29
30	31					

APRIL
M	T	W	T	F	S	S
		1	2	3	4	5
6	7	8	9	10	11	12
13	14	15	16	17	18	19
20	21	22	23	24	25	26
27	28	29	30			

MAY
M	T	W	T	F	S	S
				1	2	3
4	5	6	7	8	9	10
11	12	13	14	15	16	17
18	19	20	21	22	23	24
25	26	27	28	29	30	31

JUNE
M	T	W	T	F	S	S
1	2	3	4	5	6	7
8	9	10	11	12	13	14
15	16	17	18	19	20	21
22	23	24	25	26	27	28
29	30					

JULY
M	T	W	T	F	S	S
		1	2	3	4	5
6	7	8	9	10	11	12
13	14	15	16	17	18	19
20	21	22	23	24	25	26
27	28	29	30	31		

AUGUST
M	T	W	T	F	S	S
					1	2
3	4	5	6	7	8	9
10	11	12	13	14	15	16
17	18	19	20	21	22	23
24	25	26	27	28	29	30
31						

SEPTEMBER
M	T	W	T	F	S	S
	1	2	3	4	5	6
7	8	9	10	11	12	13
14	15	16	17	18	19	20
21	22	23	24	25	26	27
28	29	30				

OCTOBER
M	T	W	T	F	S	S
			1	2	3	4
5	6	7	8	9	10	11
12	13	14	15	16	17	18
19	20	21	22	23	24	25
26	27	28	29	30	31	

NOVEMBER
M	T	W	T	F	S	S
						1
2	3	4	5	6	7	8
9	10	11	12	13	14	15
16	17	18	19	20	21	22
23	24	25	26	27	28	29
30						

DECEMBER
M	T	W	T	F	S	S
	1	2	3	4	5	6
7	8	9	10	11	12	13
14	15	16	17	18	19	20
21	22	23	24	25	26	27
28	29	30	31			

CALENDAR 2016

JANUARY
M	T	W	T	F	S	S
				1	2	3
4	5	6	7	8	9	10
11	12	13	14	15	16	17
18	19	20	21	22	23	24
25	26	27	28	29	30	31

FEBRUARY
M	T	W	T	F	S	S
1	2	3	4	5	6	7
8	9	10	11	12	13	14
15	16	17	18	19	20	21
22	23	24	25	26	27	28
29						

MARCH
M	T	W	T	F	S	S
	1	2	3	4	5	6
7	8	9	10	11	12	13
14	15	16	17	18	19	20
21	22	23	24	25	26	27
28	29	30	31			

APRIL
M	T	W	T	F	S	S
				1	2	3
4	5	6	7	8	9	10
11	12	13	14	15	16	17
18	19	20	21	22	23	24
25	26	27	28	29	30	

MAY
M	T	W	T	F	S	S
						1
2	3	4	5	6	7	8
9	10	11	12	13	14	15
16	17	18	19	20	21	22
23	24	25	26	27	28	29
30	31					

JUNE
M	T	W	T	F	S	S
		1	2	3	4	5
6	7	8	9	10	11	12
13	14	15	16	17	18	19
20	21	22	23	24	25	26
27	28	29	30			

JULY
M	T	W	T	F	S	S
				1	2	3
4	5	6	7	8	9	10
11	12	13	14	15	16	17
18	19	20	21	22	23	24
25	26	27	28	29	30	31

AUGUST
M	T	W	T	F	S	S
1	2	3	4	5	6	7
8	9	10	11	12	13	14
15	16	17	18	19	20	21
22	23	24	25	26	27	28
29	30	31				

SEPTEMBER
M	T	W	T	F	S	S
			1	2	3	4
5	6	7	8	9	10	11
12	13	14	15	16	17	18
19	20	21	22	23	24	25
26	27	28	29	30		

OCTOBER
M	T	W	T	F	S	S
					1	2
3	4	5	6	7	8	9
10	11	12	13	14	15	16
17	18	19	20	21	22	23
24	25	26	27	28	29	30
31						

NOVEMBER
M	T	W	T	F	S	S
	1	2	3	4	5	6
7	8	9	10	11	12	13
14	15	16	17	18	19	20
21	22	23	24	25	26	27
28	29	30				

DECEMBER
M	T	W	T	F	S	S
			1	2	3	4
5	6	7	8	9	10	11
12	13	14	15	16	17	18
19	20	21	22	23	24	25
26	27	28	29	30	31	

GARDENS AND WILDLIFE

Gardens as a network form an important ecosystem. An ecosystem is an interdependent and dynamic system of living organisms which is considered together with the physical and geographical environment. Ecosystems are interdependent because everything in a garden depends on everything else.

The garden ecosystem is extremely variable, thereby offering year-round interest. Gardens can offer a large number of animals the perfect conditions for different stages of their life cycle. Insects may prefer sunny, sheltered spots to forage and mate in, but their larvae may need to live in water or in rotting vegetation. The large range of garden wildlife is there because of gardening, not despite it.

Because of the nature of gardens, groups of species that exploit a network of gardens' resources can find abundance over a longer time period, compared to what a single natural site can offer. Even gardens that are managed without regard for wildlife still offer some benefit, especially when they are considered as part of the total garden network. Even without simulated 'wild' habitats, gardens are living, diverse ecosystems in their own right. No garden is too small to provide some benefit to wildlife. Many visiting animals can actually be residents of neighbouring gardens. It is the garden network that is of overall importance to wildlife, forming the larger garden ecosystem.

City gardens are important corridors that facilitate the safe movement of birds, butterflies and other wildlife. Wildlife-friendly gardens don't need to be messy, with an abundance of stinging nettles. All gardens offer some resource to certain species; however, with a little thought and planning, every garden can be of great benefit to a much wider range of species. Look around your local area and see what type of habitat is missing and whether it is possible for you to provide it: perhaps a pond, nest boxes, decaying wood or an undisturbed leaf pile? The more diverse the habitats that are provided, the greater will be the variety of birds and wildlife visiting your garden.

The RHS recognizes and actively promotes the valuable contribution that gardens make to wildlife, believing that with thoughtful management it is possible to enhance the wildlife potential in any garden without compromising the gardener's enjoyment of it. For more information visit: www.rhs.org.uk and www.wildaboutgardens.org

JOBS FOR THE MONTH

- Hang bird feeders and put out food on the ground and bird table.
- Make sure the bird bath is topped up and the water is not frozen.
- Regularly clean the bird bath and table.
- Make sure the pond does not freeze. Never crack or hit the ice; instead fill a saucepan with hot water and rest it on the ice until a hole has melted.
- Leave out food for hedgehogs (*see* Week 36).

INSECTS

It pays to be insect-friendly in your planting as insects are vital to maintain a garden's ecosystem. Some will eat your garden pests, others will be a food source for birds and small mammals and others are important pollinators.

- Plant evergreen shrubs to provide winter hibernation sites for butterflies and moths.
- Plant Sea lavender, buddlejas, *Centranthus ruber* and *Lychnis* to attract day-flying moths.
- Night-flowering nectar-rich plants will attract nocturnal moths.
- Plant tall plants and dense bushes for spiders and leave areas of the garden undisturbed.

BIRDS

Winter is a tough time for birds as natural resources are at their lowest. Supplying food regularly will encourage birds to visit your garden. Birds appreciate variety so put out mealworms and fat balls as well as bird seed. Different types of food will appeal to different birds (*see* Week 18); as will where food is placed in the garden (*see* Week 23).

- You can make your own fat balls but avoid fat from cooking and polyunsaturated margarines and vegetable oils as they are unsuitable. Lard and beef suet can be used.
- Fill holes and cracks of a post or tree with suet to encourage more agile birds.
- If scattering food on the ground, vary the location every few days and space it out to avoid competition between birds. If there is snow on the ground, remove it before placing out the food.
- Always remove any nylon mesh bags around fat balls as these can trap and injure birds.
- Remove stale or mouldy food from the bird table promptly as it can be a breeding ground for salmonella, which can be fatal for some birds.

DECEMBER AND JANUARY 2015

Monday 29

Tuesday 30

New Year's Eve

Wednesday 31

New Year's Day
Holiday, UK, Republic of Ireland,
Canada, USA, Australia and New Zealand

Thursday 1

Holiday, Scotland and New Zealand

Friday 2

Saturday 3

Sunday 4

JANUARY

5 *Monday*   *Full Moon*

6 *Tuesday*   Epiphany

7 *Wednesday*

8 *Thursday*

9 *Friday*

10 *Saturday*

11 *Sunday*

Eurasian Bullfinch (*Pyrrhula pyrrhula*) adult male, perched on teasel seedhead.

JANUARY

Monday 12

Last Quarter

Tuesday 13

Wednesday 14

Thursday 15

Friday 16

Saturday 17

Sunday 18

Lesser Redpoll (*Carduelis cabaret*) adult male, feeding on seeds from burdock seedhead.

JANUARY

---

19 *Monday*   Holiday, USA (Martin Luther King Jnr Day)

---

20 *Tuesday*   *New Moon*

---

21 *Wednesday*

---

22 *Thursday*

---

23 *Friday*

---

24 *Saturday*

---

25 *Sunday*

European Hedgehog (*Erinaceus europaeus*) adult, hibernating amongst flowerpots.

JANUARY AND FEBRUARY

Holiday, Australia (Australia Day)   *Monday* 26

First Quarter   *Tuesday* 27

Wednesday 28

Thursday 29

Friday 30

Saturday 31

Sunday 1

Blue Tit (*Parus caeruleus*) raising its crest.

FEBRUARY

2 *Monday*

3 *Tuesday*   *Full Moon*

4 *Wednesday*

5 *Thursday*

6 *Friday*   Accession of Queen Elizabeth II
                                                                Holiday, New Zealand (Waitangi Day)

7 *Saturday*

8 *Sunday*

'Keep an eye out for birds beginning to gather nesting materials.'

POND LIFE

The smallest pond will attract dragonflies, damselflies and other insects, as well as newts, toads and frogs. Frogs and toads will eat your slugs and snails. A pond or small water feature is an important water source for all wildlife.

- Late winter is a great time to put in a pond and you may get your first toads by the spring.
- Choose a sunny location with sufficient planting around the edges to provide a safe 'corridor' to hibernation areas, as well as a food source. A nearby logpile will provide welcome shelter and a food larder.
- Avoid cobbles or paving around the edges as this can heat up quickly, which can be lethal for young amphibians crossing to reach shady areas.
- Ensure easy access to the water. This can be with a sloping side or strategically placed rocks and stones. Birds like a large flat rock sitting just beneath the surface for easy drinking and bathing.
- Connect a rainwater butt to the pond so it fills automatically.
- Vary the depth of water so there are shallow areas as well as deeper water, which will help some aquatic insects survive cold spells.
- Consider pond safety and take the necessary precautions for any young children around the pond.

JOBS FOR THE MONTH

- Put up nesting boxes for birds (*see* Week 32). Research different sizes, shapes and types if you want to attract specific birds to the garden.
- Keep bird feeders topped up and put food out on the ground and bird table. Avoid foods that could cause choking in young fledglings.
- Keep the bird bath topped up and unfrozen for part of the day.
- Regularly clean the bird bath and table; dispose of old food.
- Make sure the bird bath and table are kept clear of snow.
- Put out hedgehog food (*see* Week 36).
- Keep the pond from freezing over (*see* Week 1).

BEES

Bees are under threat but are essential pollinators in the garden.

- Plan planting to include flowers from February through to November and plant in clumps.
- Avoid using pesticides and if you have to, spray in the evening.
- Avoid double or multi-petaled cultivars which can lack pollen and/or nectar or be difficult to reach.

FEBRUARY

Monday 9

Tuesday 10

Wednesday 11

Last Quarter

Thursday 12

Friday 13

Valentine's Day

Saturday 14

Sunday 15

Chaffinch (*Fringilla coelebs*) adult male, perched on umbellifer stem.

FEBRUARY

16 *Monday* — Holiday, USA (Presidents' Day)

17 *Tuesday* — Shrove Tuesday

18 *Wednesday* — *New Moon*
Ash Wednesday

19 *Thursday* — Chinese New Year

20 *Friday*

21 *Saturday*

22 *Sunday*

Great Tit (*Parus major*) adult, feeding on fat ball mixture in coconut shell.

FEBRUARY AND MARCH

Monday 23

Tuesday 24

First Quarter

Wednesday 25

Thursday 26

Friday 27

Saturday 28

St David's Day

Sunday 1

Eurasian Red Squirrel (*Sciurus vulgaris*) adult, feeding.

2 *Monday*

3 *Tuesday*

4 *Wednesday*

5 *Thursday*   *Full Moon*

6 *Friday*

7 *Saturday*

8 *Sunday*

'Look out for amphibian spawn in ponds. Frog spawn is in clumps; toad spawn is in long double strands and newt spawn is laid individually.'

JOBS FOR THE MONTH

- Put up nesting boxes for birds (*see* Week 32).
- Top up bird feeders and put food out on the ground and bird table.
- Avoid chunky foods, such as peanuts, that might cause young fledglings to choke.
- Keep the bird bath topped up and clean it regularly.
- Put out hedgehog food (*see* Week 36).
- Make your pond more wildlife friendly (*see* Week 6).
- Sow or plant a wildflower meadow.
- Hang a bat nesting box.
- Create log and twig piles from prunings and felled trees. This will provide protection and debris for nests, and shelter for small mammals and some birds.
- Remove any netting placed over the pond to protect it from autumn leaf fall.

CHOOSING A BIRD TABLE

A bird table can be a simple tray, with or without a roof. A raised edge will retain food and a gap in each corner will allow water to drain away and facilitate cleaning. Avoid fancy designs that are difficult to clean. Choose a location bearing in mind predators such as cats.

TEN WAYS TO ENCOURAGE WILDLIFE

- Plant native species to support local wildlife; crab apples, hawthorn, honeysuckle, rowan and sunflowers are all popular with birds.
- Allow some of your plants to go to seed.
- Plant berry-producing plants for a winter food source.
- Weed by hand as much as possible to avoid using pesticides.
- Mulch to suppress weeds and also provide insect habitats.
- Create wildlife 'corridors' along the edges and across your garden. These can be created by simply leaving the grass and planting uncut.
- Create a pond or water feature (*see* Week 6).
- Create a compost heap to generate insects for bats and other small mammals, as well as a hibernation site
- Replace a fence with a native hedge to provide safe passage for wildlife as well as a hibernation and nesting site and food source.

MARCH

Commonwealth Day

Monday 9

Tuesday 10

Wednesday 11

Thursday 12

Last Quarter

Friday 13

Saturday 14

Mother's Day, UK and Republic of Ireland

Sunday 15

European Robin (*Erithacus rubecula*) adult

MARCH

16 *Monday*

17 *Tuesday*

St Patrick's Day
Holiday, Northern Ireland and Republic of Ireland

18 *Wednesday*

19 *Thursday*

20 *Friday*

New Moon
Vernal Equinox (Spring begins)

21 *Saturday*

22 *Sunday*

Common frog (*Rana temporaria*) with frog spawn

MARCH

Monday 23

Tuesday 24

Wednesday 25

Thursday 26

First Quarter

Friday 27

Saturday 28

British Summer Time begins
Palm Sunday

Sunday 29

Holly Blue (*Celastrina argiolus*) adult, resting on European Holly (*Ilex aquifolium*) berries.

30 *Monday*

31 *Tuesday*

1 *Wednesday*

2 *Thursday*

Maundy Thursday

3 *Friday*

Good Friday
Holiday, UK, Canada, Australia and New Zealand

4 *Saturday*

Full Moon
First day of Passover (Pesach)
Holiday, Australia (Easter Saturday)

5 *Sunday*

Easter Sunday

Orange-tip Butterfly (*Anthocharis cardamines*) adult male and female, resting on Ramsons (*Allium ursinum*).

'Keep an eye out for summer visitors such as willow warblers, housemartins, swifts and swallows who will start arriving.'

JOBS FOR THE MONTH
- Put up nesting boxes for birds (*see* Week 32).
- Top up bird feeders and put food out on the ground and bird table (*see* Week 18 and Week 23).
- Avoid chunky foods that might cause young fledglings to choke.
- Keep the bird bath topped up.
- Put out hedgehog food (*see* Week 36).
- Make your pond more wildlife friendly (*see* Week 6).
- Create log, twig and/or rock piles to provide shelter for wildlife.
- Plant annuals and perennials to attract insects.
- Plant single flowers to encourage beneficial insects into the garden.

INSECTS
Wildlife encompasses more than birds, bees and butterflies. Every living thing has a role to play in your garden's ecosystem. Many of these 'good' insects are natural predators as well as playing their own role in the food chain.
- Woodlice and earthworms recycle organic matter.
- Ground beetles and centipedes will eat slugs.
- Spiders eat wasps and mosquitos.
- Ladybirds consume huge quantities of aphids as well as other insects and larvae that can damage your plants.
- Lacewing larvae feed on aphids, mites and other small insects.
- Hoverfly larvae are one of the first to become active in the early spring and eat aphids, particularly those in places other beneficial insects can't get to.

BATS
Bats begin roosting now. Bats eat insects including garden pests or nuisance insects like mosquitoes. Bats are a good indication of a healthy, insect-rich environment. There are 17 species of bats in Britain but their numbers have declined. The more common species likely to be seen in the garden are the common pipistrelle, soprano pipistrelle, brown long-eared bat, noctule and Daubenton's bat.

APRIL

Easter Monday,
Holiday UK (exc. Scotland), Republic of Ireland,
Australia and New Zealand

Monday 6

Tuesday 7

Wednesday 8

Thursday 9

Friday 10

Saturday 11

Last Quarter

Sunday 12

APRIL

13 *Monday*

14 *Tuesday*

15 *Wednesday*

16 *Thursday*

17 *Friday*

18 *Saturday*

New Moon

19 *Sunday*

Smooth Newt (*Triturus vulgaris*) adult male, breeding colours

APRIL

Monday 20

Birthday of Queen Elizabeth II

Tuesday 21

Wednesday 22

St George's Day

Thursday 23

Friday 24

First Quarter
Anzac Day
Holiday, Australia (Anzac Day)

Saturday 25

Sunday 26

European Rabbit (*Oryctolagus cuniculus*) young

APRIL AND MAY

27 *Monday*   Holiday, New Zealand (Anzac Day)

28 *Tuesday*

29 *Wednesday*

30 *Thursday*

1 *Friday*

2 *Saturday*

3 *Sunday*

'Look for tadpoles developing their adult 'frog-legs'. You may see them emerging from the pond and going into the undergrowth.'

MAMMALS
Hedgehog litters are being born and parents may come out to forage at night.

JOBS FOR THE MONTH
- Put up nesting boxes (*see* Week 32).
- Avoid disturbing nesting birds in garden shrubs and hedges.
- Top up bird feeders and put food out on the ground and bird table. Avoid chunky foods that might cause young fledglings to choke (*see* right).
- Regularly top up and clean out the bird bath and table.
- Make your pond more wildlife friendly (*see* Week 6).
- Remove weeds from ponds, leaving them on the side for twenty-four hours to allow trapped creatures to return to the water before adding them to the compost heap.
- Create log, twig and/or rock piles to create shelter for wildlife.
- Choose annuals and perennials to attract insects.
- Leave informal hedges un-trimmed for a while to provide food and shelter for wildlife.

CHOOSING BIRD FOOD
Bird food need not be shop bought or expensive and you can make your own (*see* Week 1). As well as providing birds with a balanced diet, consider different species' requirements particularly if you want to see more of a particular species in your garden.

Dunnocks crumbs of bread and fat and small seed from the ground

Finches berry cakes

Goldfinches niger seeds

Robins live mealworms

Sparrows, finches and nuthatches sunflower heads

Starlings peanut cakes

Tits insect cakes

Thrushes and blackbirds fruit such as over-ripe apples, raisins and song-bird mix scattered on the ground.

Wrens prefer natural foods but will take fat, bread and seed in harsh winter weather.

MAY

Full Moon
Early Spring Holiday, UK
Holiday, Republic of Ireland

Monday 4

Tuesday 5

Wednesday 6

Thursday 7

Friday 8

Saturday 9

Mother's Day,
USA, Canada, Australia and New Zealand

Sunday 10

European Robin (*Erithacus rubecula*) adult, feeding chicks.

MAY

11 *Monday*   Last Quarter

12 *Tuesday*

13 *Wednesday*

14 *Thursday*   Ascension Day

15 *Friday*

16 *Saturday*

17 *Sunday*

Small garden pond for amphibians and insects

MAY

New Moon
Holiday, Canada (Victoria Day)

Monday 18

Tuesday 19

Wednesday 20

Thursday 21

Friday 22

Saturday 23

Whit Sunday
Feast of Weeks (Shavuot)

Sunday 24

Hoverflies (*Eupeodes corollae*) on a globe thistle 'Veitch's Blue' (*Echinops ritro*)

MAY

---

25 *Monday*

First Quarter
Spring Holiday, UK
Holiday, USA (Memorial Day)

---

26 *Tuesday*

---

27 *Wednesday*

---

28 *Thursday*

---

29 *Friday*

---

30 *Saturday*

---

31 *Sunday*

Trinity Sunday

Green-veined White (*Pieris napi*) adult, resting on Bluebell (*Hyacinthoides non-scripta*) flower.

'Adult frogs, toads and newts start leaving the pond when the ground is damp.'

JOBS FOR THE MONTH

- Continue to put out food for birds on a regular basis, avoiding chunky foods that might cause young fledglings to choke.
- Consider having a bird bath as it can be a vital source of drinking water for birds. Birds also like to bathe all year. Always clean it regularly and keep it topped up.
- Build a 'ladybird hotel' using bundles of hollow stems or twigs.
- Put up a bat nesting box.
- Put out hedgehog food (*see* Week 36).
- Thin out, cut back or divide excessive new growth on aquatic plants.
- Create log, twig and/or rock piles to provide shelter for small mammals and insects.
- Use wildlife-friendly slug pellets.
- Mow spring-flowering meadows once bulb foliage has died down.
- Control weeds by mowing recently established perennial meadows.

POND CARE

Aerate the water with a hose and spray attachment. Adding oxygen will aid the fish. Remove dead foliage and blooms.

INSECTS

Hoverflies are in abundance. These harmless insects are good pest controllers, as are wasps. They are also useful pollinators.

MAMMALS

Young mammals are beginning to explore beyond the nest.

PLACING BIRD FOOD

Birds have different feeding requirements (*see* Week 18) so think about *where* you are placing food.

Dunnocks ground feeders
Chaffinches bird tables and the ground
Greenfinches anywhere including hanging feeders
Robins bird tables and ground
Sparrows eat anywhere
Thrushes ground feeders but will take from a table
Tits and Nuthatches prefer hanging feeders but also bird tables
Wrens seldom visit feeders or bird tables as they prefer natural food sources.

JUNE

Holiday, Republic of Ireland
Holiday, New Zealand (The Queen's Birthday)

Monday 1

Full Moon
Coronation Day

Tuesday 2

Wednesday 3

Corpus Christi

Thursday 4

Friday 5

Saturday 6

Sunday 7

JUNE

---

8 *Monday*   Holiday, Australia (The Queen's Birthday)

---

9 *Tuesday*   *Last Quarter*

---

10 *Wednesday*

---

11 *Thursday*

---

12 *Friday*

---

13 *Saturday*   The Queen's Official Birthday
                                                          (subject to confirmation)

---

14 *Sunday*

Buff-tailed Bumblebee (*Bombus terrestris*) queen visiting Japanese quince flowers.

JUNE

Monday 15

New Moon

Tuesday 16

Wednesday 17

First day of Ramadan
(subject to sighting of the moon)

Thursday 18

Friday 19

Saturday 20

Summer Solstice (Summer begins)
Father's Day, UK, Republic of Ireland, USA and Canada

Sunday 21

Elephant Hawkmoth (*Deilephila elpenor*) adult, resting on honeysuckle stem.

JUNE

22 *Monday*

23 *Tuesday*

24 *Wednesday*   *First Quarter*

25 *Thursday*

26 *Friday*

27 *Saturday*

28 *Sunday*

'This is the season for bat watching.'

JOBS FOR THE MONTH

- Top up bird feeders and put food out on the ground and bird tables (*see* Week 18 and Week 23).
- Avoid chunky foods that might cause young fledglings to choke.
- Keep the bird bath topped up and clean regularly.
- Plant marigolds around the vegetable patch to attract hoverflies for pest control.
- Put out hedgehog food (*see* Week 36).
- Construct a hedgehog hibernation box for the coming winter.
- Plant annuals and perennials to attract insects.
- Trim hedges less frequently to allow wildlife to shelter and feed in them.
- Leave nesting birds undisturbed in garden shrubs and trees.
- Avoid deadheading roses that produce hips, as these are a valuable food source.
- Top up ponds and water features if necessary. Aerating the water using a hose with spray attachment adds oxygen, which will help the fish.
- Remove dead foliage and blooms from aquatic plants.

BATS

Bats are excellent pest controllers. All bats are legally protected in Britain and this protection extends to their roosting and hibernation sites. During the day bats hide in dark places like hollow trees so retain old trees with cavities in the trunk where possible. This time of year is the best time to go bat-watching in the evening. Generally they will seek their own spaces but you can provide bat boxes.

- Compost heaps and ponds will generate the type of insects bats like to eat.
- Grow plants with flowers that are likely to attract moths and other night-flying insects. White or pale-coloured flowers are more likely to be seen by nocturnal insects.
- Be insect tolerant. Spare a few caterpillars to feed a bat!
- Avoid using pesticides where possible.

INSECTS

July is flying ant season. Also you will now be seeing an abundance of harmless hoverflies. They are good garden pest catchers. Wasps are also good pest controllers as they eat flies and grubs. They are also useful flower pollinators.

JUNE AND JULY

Monday 29

Tuesday 30

Holiday, Canada (Canada Day)

Wednesday 1

Full Moon

Thursday 2

Holiday, USA

Friday 3

Independence Day, USA

Sunday 5

6 *Monday*

7 *Tuesday*

8 *Wednesday*   *Last Quarter*

9 *Thursday*

10 *Friday*

11 *Saturday*

12 *Sunday*   *Battle of the Boyne*

JULY

Holiday, Northern Ireland (Battle of the Boyne)

Monday 13

Tuesday 14

St Swithin's Day

Wednesday 15

New Moon

Thursday 16

Eid al-Fitr (end of Ramadan)
(subject to sighting of the moon)

Friday 17

Saturday 18

Sunday 19

Painted Lady (*Vanessa cardui*) adult, emerging from pupa, hanging from stinging nettle leaf.

JULY

20 *Monday*

21 *Tuesday*

22 *Wednesday*

23 *Thursday*

24 *Friday*   *First Quarter*

25 *Saturday*

26 *Sunday*

JULY AND AUGUST

Monday 27

Tuesday 28

Wednesday 29

Thursday 30

Full Moon   *Friday* 31

Saturday 1

Sunday 2

Common Field Grasshopper (*Chorthippus brunneus*) adult

AUGUST

3 *Monday*   Holiday, Scotland
                                        Holiday, Republic of Ireland

4 *Tuesday*

5 *Wednesday*

6 *Thursday*

7 *Friday*   *Last Quarter*

8 *Saturday*

9 *Sunday*

'At this time of year many birds enjoy 'dust-bathing' as well as splashing about in a bird bath or pond.'

JOBS FOR THE MONTH

- Top up bird feeders and put food out on the ground and bird tables.
- Avoid chunky foods that might cause young fledglings to choke (*see* Week 18 and Week 23).
- Keep the bird bath topped up.
- Clean bird baths and tables regularly.
- Plant marigolds around the vegetable patch for pest control.
- Put out hedgehog food (*see* Week 36).
- Make a hedgehog hibernation box.
- Plant annuals and perennials to attract insects.
- Trim hedges less frequently to allow wildlife to shelter and feed in them.
- Leave nesting birds undisturbed in garden shrubs and trees.
- Allow seed heads to develop on some plants as a food source.

HABITATS FOR BIRDS

As natural habitats are destroyed installing or building a nest box is another way to encourage birds to your garden. The main criteria is that they are weatherproof and safe and secure, although certain species favour particular types and locations.

- Wood is the best material but not plywood or chipboard.
- Treat the outside only with a water-based wood preservative (don't use creosote).
- Position away from potential predators and from any feeding area. Angle slightly down to allow water run-off.
- Birds are territorial so avoid multiple boxes in a small area.
- Clean out the box at the end of each breeding season. In October/ November scald the inside with boiling water to kill any parasites.
- Leave out over winter to provide shelter in harsh weather.

AUGUST

Monday 10

Tuesday 11

Wednesday 12

Thursday 13

New Moon

Friday 14

Saturday 15

Sunday 16

AUGUST

WEEK **34**

17 *Monday*

18 *Tuesday*

19 *Wednesday*

20 *Thursday*

21 *Friday*

22 *Saturday*   *First Quarter*

23 *Sunday*

Red Slug (*Arion rufus*) adult

AUGUST

Monday 24

Tuesday 25

Wednesday 26

Thursday 27

Friday 28

Full Moon

Saturday 29

Sunday 30

Barn Owl (*Tyto alba*) chicks, perched at entrance to nest in tree stump, awaiting parents return with food.

---

31 *Monday*   Holiday, UK (exc. Scotland)

---

1 *Tuesday*

---

2 *Wednesday*

---

3 *Thursday*

---

4 *Friday*

---

5 *Saturday*   *Last Quarter*

---

6 *Sunday*   Father's Day, Australia and New Zealand

'Planting autumn flowering plants will support bees and butterflies.'

JOBS FOR THE MONTH

- Continue to feed birds, avoiding chunky foods that might cause young fledglings to choke (*see* Week 18 and Week 23).
- Keep the bird bath topped up and clean regularly.
- Construct a hedgehog hibernation box.
- Trim hedges less frequently to create shelter for wildlife. They can also be an important food source.
- Give meadows a final cut before winter.
- Cover the pond surface with netting to stop fallen leaves from entering.

HEDGEHOGS

Hedgehogs are natural pest controllers and eat snails, slugs, beetles, caterpillars and worms. They appreciate supplementary feeding in winter but give them dog or cat food and avoid bread and milk. Hedges offer them some protection when they wander and they like thick dense undergrowth and varying lengths of grass. They hibernate in leaf piles, compost heaps or under hedges or sheds.

BUTTERFLIES

There are 59 butterfly species resident in Britain, plus up to 30 others that are migrant visitors from continental Europe. In the garden you are most likely to see Red Admiral, Peacock, Brimstone, Painted Lady, Comma, Green-veined White, Small Cabbage White and Large Cabbage White. You may sometimes see Orange-tip, Speckled Wood, Meadow Brown, Small Copper and Holly Blue. The Small Tortoiseshell used to be commonly seen but its numbers are in decline.

- Butterflies feed on nectar so plant a range of suitable flowers from March through to October–November.
- In late summer butterflies like Red Admiral and Painted Lady will appreciate fallen fruit left on the ground.
- To support the butterfly you need to look after the young caterpillars so research the plants that will best support them. For example, native ivy supports both caterpillars and adult butterflies.

SEPTEMBER

Holiday, Canada (Labour Day)
Holiday, USA (Labor Day)

Monday 7

Tuesday 8

Wednesday 9

Thursday 10

Friday 11

Saturday 12

New Moon

Sunday 13

Green Lacewing (*Chrysopa perla*) adult

SEPTEMBER

14 *Monday*   Jewish New Year (Rosh Hashanah)

15 *Tuesday*

16 *Wednesday*

17 *Thursday*

18 *Friday*

19 *Saturday*

20 *Sunday*

Cutters filled with berries for birds.

SEPTEMBER

First Quarter

Monday 21

Tuesday 22

Autumnal Equinox (Autumn begins)
Day of Atonement (Yom Kippur)

Wednesday 23

Thursday 24

Friday 25

Saturday 26

Sunday 27

Wood Mouse (*Apodemus sylvaticus*) adult, feeding on fallen blackberry.

28 *Monday*

Full Moon
First day of Tabernacles (Succoth)

---

29 *Tuesday*

Michaelmas Day

---

30 *Wednesday*

---

1 *Thursday*

---

2 *Friday*

---

3 *Saturday*

---

4 *Sunday*

Last Quarter

'Look out for winter migrants starting to arrive from colder, northern regions.'

JOBS FOR THE MONTH

- Top up bird feeders and put food out on the ground and bird tables. All feeds, including peanuts, are safe, as the breeding season is now over.
- Keep the bird bath topped up and clean regularly.
- Put out hedgehog food (*see* Week 36).
- Construct a hedgehog hibernation box.
- Where possible leave seed heads standing to provide food and shelter for wildlife. If possible leave mature ivy uncut to flower.
- Make a leaf pile for hibernating mammals and overwintering ground-feeding birds; add in some logs to widen the appeal for a greater range of insects; or build a 'bug hotel'.

BIRDS

Look out for redwings, bramblings and fieldfares visiting the garden but don't be surprised if your feeder is untouched. Birds will still be enjoying natural food, which is their preference. However, you can do your bit by making sure your garden offers a natural food 'cafe'.

MAMMALS

Mammals start going into hibernation. If you have a hedgehog hibernating box site it in a quiet shady part of the garden. Leave piles of old leaves undisturbed for small mammals. Take care when turning compost heaps as frogs, toads and small animals may be living there.

INSECTS

Insects need a helping hand to survive the cold weather too. There are some simple things that can be done to help.

- Leaving herbaceous and hollow stemmed plants unpruned until early spring will provide homes for over-wintering insects.
- Plant autumn daisies for butterflies and bees as now there are few other plants in flower for them to feed on. Mature ivy flowers late, providing an excellent nectar source for wildlife.
- Although caterpillars will eat your plants they will grow into butterflies that will help with pollination (and will look beautiful too). Top favourite food for caterpillars includes stinging nettle, thistle, wild carrot, bird's-foot trefoil, buckthorn and blackthorn.

OCTOBER

Monday 5

Tuesday 6

Wednesday 7

Thursday 8

Friday 9

Saturday 10

Sunday 11

Pale Tussock Caterpillar on Malus

OCTOBER

---

12 *Monday*   Holiday, Canada (Thanksgiving)
                                                    Holiday, USA (Columbus Day)

---

13 *Tuesday*   *New Moon*

---

14 *Wednesday*

---

15 *Thursday*   Islamic New Year

---

16 *Friday*

---

17 *Saturday*

---

18 *Sunday*

Seven-spot Ladybird (*Coccinella septempunctata*) adult, resting on Rowan (*Sorbus aucuparia*) leaf.

OCTOBER

Monday 19

First Quarter

Tuesday 20

Wednesday 21

Thursday 22

Friday 23

Saturday 24

British Summer Time ends

Sunday 25

Cranefly (*Tipula oleracea*) adult female, resting amongst fothergilla leaves.

---

26 *Monday*

Holiday, Republic of Ireland
Holiday, New Zealand (Labour Day)

---

27 *Tuesday*

Full Moon

---

28 *Wednesday*

---

29 *Thursday*

---

30 *Friday*

---

31 *Saturday*

Halloween

---

1 *Sunday*

All Saints' Day

Lesser Spotted Woodpecker (*Dendrocopos minor*)

'Plant evergreen shrubs to help butterflies and moths survive the winter.'

MOTHS

Although perhaps not as instantly appealing as butterflies, moths have an important role to play in the garden. There are over 2,500 species in Britain. The presence of moths – or their absence – is an important indicator of the health of the environment as they are particularly sensitive to change.

- Both adult moths and their caterpillars are an important food source for other wildlife including spiders, frogs, toads, lizards, shrews, hedgehogs, bats, owls and birds. Day moths are plant pollinators. Moth caterpillars are a particularly important food source for the young of blue tits, great tits, robins and other birds.
- Plant sea lavender, buddlejas, *Centranthus ruber* and *Lychnis* to attract day-flying moths.
- Plant night-flowering, nectar-rich plants and white or pale-coloured flowering plants to encourage nocturnal moths.
- Plant oak, birch, willow, hawthorn, hornbeam and lady's bedstraw to support moth caterpillars.
- Plant evergreen shrubs to provide winter hibernation sites for butterflies and moths.
- Leave longer grasses, thistles and knapweeds in the garden.
- Leave hedges untrimmed where possible.

JOBS FOR THE MONTH

- All bird feeds are now safe, so continue to put food out regularly.
- Keep the bird bath topped up and clean regularly.
- Make a hedgehog hibernation box.
- Leave seed heads standing to provide food and shelter for wildlife.
- Leave mature ivy uncut to flower. The nectar is a food source for insects.
- Make a leaf pile for hibernating mammals and overwintering ground-feeding birds.
- Empty and clean out nesting boxes with boiling water. When thoroughly dry, place a handful of wood shavings inside. They may provide winter shelter. It is illegal to remove unhatched eggs except between November and January.
- Regularly shake off leaves from nets over ponds. Rake out leaves from ponds that are not netted.

NOVEMBER

Monday 2

Last Quarter

Tuesday 3

Wednesday 4

Guy Fawkes

Thursday 5

Friday 6

Saturday 7

Remembrance Sunday

Sunday 8

NOVEMBER

---

9 *Monday*

---

10 *Tuesday*

---

11 *Wednesday*

New Moon
Holiday, USA (Veterans' Day)
Holiday, Canada (Remembrance Day)

---

12 *Thursday*

---

13 *Friday*

---

14 *Saturday*

---

15 *Sunday*

Crested Tit (*Lophophanes cristatus*) adult, perched on pine twig.

NOVEMBER

Monday 16

Tuesday 17

Wednesday 18

First Quarter

Thursday 19

Friday 20

Saturday 21

Sunday 22

Ilex aquifolium 'Golden van Tol'. The red winter berries are a rich source of food for birds.

NOVEMBER

23 *Monday*

24 *Tuesday*

25 *Wednesday*   *Full Moon*

26 *Thursday*   Holiday, USA (Thanksgiving)

27 *Friday*

28 *Saturday*

29 *Sunday*   First Sunday in Advent

Fieldfare (*Turdus pilaris*) adult, feeding on European Holly (*Ilex aquifolium*) fruit.

'When collecting foliage for Christmas decorations remember to leave some holly berries for the birds!'

JOBS FOR THE MONTH

- Top up bird feeders and put food out on the ground and bird tables (*see* Week 18 and Week 23). Once a feeding regime is established try and keep to it, as this will encourage birds to return.
- All bird feed, including peanuts, are safe, as the breeding season is over.
- Keep the bird bath topped up and ice free (*see* Week 1).
- Clean bird baths and tables regularly.
- Where possible leave seed heads standing to provide food and shelter for wildlife.
- If possible leave mature ivy uncut to flower.
- Make a leaf pile for hibernating mammals and over wintering ground-feeding birds.

BIRDS

Now is the time to make sure you are including fat in any food you put out for birds. Make sure any fat blocks are in wire cages and not plastic nets which can be harmful. Wrens and other small birds appreciate finely chopped bacon rind and grated cheese. Put out food regularly so birds don't waste vital energy on visiting when there is no food.

PLAN FOR VARYING HABITATS

Winter is a good time for planning your garden to support and encourage wildlife. Creating a variety of different habitats will suport the needs of all levels of the food chain. Key habitats to include if possible are a lawn, trees, shrubs, flowers and water. Consider what habitats are available in neighbouring gardens and if there are any gaps, that could be a place to start.

- Consider planting early- and late-flowering plants to help bridge the lean period before and after summer.
- Plant a single native tree to provide a host of habitats for those at the bottom of the food chain.
- Create micro habitats such as a small patch of short grass to allow birds easy access to grubs and worms; long grass creates habitats for egg laying and over-wintering insects; a pile of logs will provide a home for insects and shelter for small mammals.
- Prune your shrubs at different times to create varied cycles of growth to benefit wildlife.

NOVEMBER AND DECEMBER

St Andrew's Day

Monday 30

Tuesday 1

Wednesday 2

Last Quarter

Thursday 3

Friday 4

Saturday 5

Hannukah begins

Sunday 6

DECEMBER

7 *Monday*

8 *Tuesday*

9 *Wednesday*

10 *Thursday*

11 *Friday*   *New Moon*

12 *Saturday*

13 *Sunday*

Eurasian Red Squirrel (*Sciurus vulgaris*) adult

DECEMBER

Monday 14

Hannukah ends

Tuesday 15

Wednesday 16

Thursday 17

First Quarter

Friday 18

Saturday 19

Sunday 20

European Goldfinch (*Carduelis carduelis*) adult, feeding on seeds from burdock seedhead.

DECEMBER

21 *Monday*

---

22 *Tuesday*

Winter Solstice (Winter begins)

---

23 *Wednesday*

---

24 *Thursday*

Christmas Eve

---

25 *Friday*

Full Moon
Christmas Day
Holiday, UK, Republic of Ireland, USA,
Canada, Australia and New Zealand

---

26 *Saturday*

Boxing Day (St Stephen's Day)

---

27 *Sunday*

Decorative moulds filled with a mixture of fat and bird seed.

DECEMBER AND JANUARY 2016

Holiday, UK, Republic of Ireland,
Canada, Australia and New Zealand

Monday 28

Tuesday 29

Wednesday 30

New Year's Eve

Thursday 31

New Year's Day
Holiday, UK, Republic of Ireland,
USA, Canada, Australia and New Zealand

Friday 1

Saturday 2

Sunday 3

European Robin (*Erithacus rubecula*) adult, feeding on apple.

NOTES